Shade and Shadow

poems

&

photographs

To Diana
I only know one of your
children monika but because
of her I know you were a
wonderful mother —
Blessings Ann

Shade and Shadow

poems

&

photographs

Ann Lovell Rowe

Mellen Poetry Press
Lewiston • Queenston • Lampeter

Library of Congress Cataloging-in-Publication Data

Rowe, Ann Lovell
    Shade and shadow : poems & photographs / Ann Lovell Rowe.
        p. cm.
    ISBN 0-7734-3547-6
    I. Title.

    PS3618.O8727S53   2004
    811'.6--dc22

                                                    2004042587

PHOTO CREDITS: All photos, including the front cover, are by the author, Ann Lovell
Rowe. The photo, "At Our Age", is printed with permission by Molly Donovan.
Family Photo with permission by Jerald Richardson.
Back Cover photo with permission by Jeff Montgomery.

Previously published work: "The Miracle of Unexpected Time"
(Columns and Photographs that appeared in the Cranford Chronicle)

Essays and Photographs: "Aspects: New Mexico"; "Aspects: Pakistan"

    The Edwin Mellen Press   The Edwin Mellen Press
            Box 450   Box 67
    Lewiston, New York   Queenston, Ontario
    USA 14092-0450   CANADA L0S 1L0

                The Edwin Mellen Press, Ltd.
                Lampeter, Ceredigion, Wales
                UNITED KINGDOM SA48 8LT

                Printed in the United States of America

To Richard…who else!

This book has had several readers in its pre-published form; they all encouraged publishing. Here are some of the readers' comments.

"There is something so unique about your poetry, in that I can really feel who you are. It is brave, revealing, and goes places we are afraid to admit to in ourselves. Your poetry, in fact, is like a photograph: it allows the usually unexpressed to be visible. In other words, if one allows herself, through the reading of your poems, she can become more visible to herself. This, in essence, defines great poetry"

—*Dina Wolff, M.A., of Authentic Publishing*

"I was invited to speak at my 50th college reunion at Smith College. At first I was reluctant because I wasn't sure what would be useful to communicate in this setting. Then a mutual friend shared these poems with me, and they helped me crystallize what was important about this period in our lives and ways in which I could share my experiences and feelings."

—*Louise White, former teacher of Political Science*

"I read the poems aloud to my husband, a thoroughly rational physicist, as we were driving across New Mexico beginning a new life as retirees and temporary vagabonds. Uncharacteristically, he responded to the feelings expressed in many of the poems, and, as a result, we were able to make an emotional connection which enhanced our relationship and this new phase of our lives."

—*Jean Munsee, retired Middle School Counselor*

Ann Lovell Rowe

"I started reading the book last night, thinking I would read just one poem. I stayed up all night reading them. You challenged me, turned on some lights about the cycle of life and family: to accept the shifting of responsibility. It is part of life. It is a gift. And motherhood for me sounds in my heart: give, give Love, love; nurture, nurture until the pitcher feels empty, until it dangles in the air, threatening to fall and shatter, not knowing where or how to refill itself

   My perception is that you've led such a full life always seeking to see in new ways, to learn....

   The pages are just one of those places you've touched"

   —Ranee Smith, Russian scholar, mother of two small children,

"Your book arrived Friday, and after supper I sat down figuring I'd do the poems and photos a few at a time, in the next weeks. At midnight I went to bed wishing there were more poems and photos. Your poems and photos are moving glimpses of the small, sometimes routine moments of a life captured in a way that reaches deep down into the emotions. I like the poem with your finger under Dick's watchband, ached with you as you looked at a home that seemed to lean into you, where once you had lived and I reflected on my own experiences with your glimpses of early marriage. Since the poems and photos were written and photographed over the years, stretching from the days when you were a young woman, they capture the freshness of each period. My 36-year-old daughter, mother of two young children, particularly liked the poem on responsibility. The photos and poems can open some in-depth sharing between my daughters and myself. And what a discussion piece for a book group!"

   —Hope Crawley, former communications and Education Director for the National Art Materials Trade Association

Shade and Shadow—poems and photographs

Contents

Ann Lovell Rowe

Introduction

For years my pens have had a strange way of collecting in one place, at the bottom of a bag, or by my bedside, on my desk, or in the kitchen. This has been an unconscious message to me: "WRITE, we are calling you."

Now suddenly while I am sitting at the piano I look up to see four clocks collecting on the end of the piano, one the old beautiful mahogany electric clock of my father's, another my own desk clock set there to adjust its time, and two radio clocks to listen to news programs while I am playing music. But four collected clocks are suddenly like my pens, calling me to SEE the time. It is time to write and to share that writing with the souls out there in the world to whom I connect.

The first time I ever wrote what I thought was a poem, "Rose colored Glasses and Bifocals," happened while I was sitting in a carrel in the college library. It just happened, on my desk. I had just had my 20th birthday, which I had found very traumatic. I had lain on my bed as the clock struck 12 and tears rolled down my cheeks and I thought, "The best times of my life are over." I later consoled myself that maybe the 20's could be good too: finish college, get a job, a husband and children. I comforted myself there would be good times ahead. This was the context of the poem.

Indeed, all those good times, and more, came, and other poems happened. That is the context of this book. Now that I have begun to collect them from small scraps of paper tucked into old diaries and journals, I am astonished that some of them exist—I have no memory of writing them. They have been difficult to look at—they

Ann Lovell Rowe

deal with deep emotions, lots of pain.

While writing poems off and on I also wrote essays and columns and news articles. Essays give one time to weave the pain and the question into more palatable images; they can contain more of the pleasures and joys for they are spread out, not as dense as the poetry.

Poems for me come from a different place way inside. When I took a Yeats poetry course, I was both deeply moved and unsettled as I learned about his life. I thought, "You have to allow yourself to go a little crazy to go deeply into the poetry place." I was just forty then, with three young sons and husband whose job kept him totally involved, and I just couldn't go crazy just then. Still, poems kept happening. During those years I would wake up in the middle of the night and go to the dining room and sit and write—it just seemed a good time, a positive insomnia.

As the years went by I wrote more prose than poetry but still poems happened, usually at the deepest darkest times.

Now it seems a time to put them out. Not easy. But too many good friends, and some strangers, have said to me, "Publish them—share them." Uneasy about exposing too much, I vacillated. Then a friend who is a Jungian analyst, said to me, "They are part of the world's soul and they will connect to other souls." Connecting to other souls is important to me.

Sometimes I intentionally write to understand the world and think that if I am not writing I am not truly alive. But then isn't just writing enough? No, not for me. The connection with others matters; it is an important part of why I write. When I began to write newspaper columns, the responses are what kept the writing flowing: the woman who stopped me on the street and said "You wrote about the raspberries!" Responses move me forward. I take heart from a comment by Frederick Beuchner, "I keep writing for that small group of faithful readers." Just a few readers are all I need.

So I have collected these poems. I would like to hold out for some happier endings to say that all is well, that the years past that are shown in these poems came to good tidy endings. I am not sure where this newer place on the late road of life will lead. Staying with the mystery feels important for now. And so . . .STILL TRUE -

THE MOST wonderful thing about writing
is being able to read back,
and be surprised at your own inspirations,
And remember them.

The most awful thing
is to read your own thoughts
and wonder why you never have them anymore.

New Jersey, 1956

Ann Lovell Rowe

BANGLADESH BASKET

I HAVE a Bangladesh gathering basket
It was a birthday gift this year.
It has another name—a sorting basket.

I filled it up with old notebooks
and thoughts on scraps of paper
often used as bookmarks.
I call them the miscellaneous.
I reach in at quiet, sacred moments
Usually early Sunday morning,
And dare to open just one.
I find there precious pieces of forgotten
    moments of my life
        almost lost to me.

I reclaim them, like a shell
One can find on the beach,
Which you can hold and touch and savor,
Then bring it back and put it on the hearth
    of the fireplace
And let it be there for you.

Santa Fe, 2002

Shade and Shadow

poems

&

photographs

I KNOW

IF I COULD be successful
I might be absurd
But I would be considered eccentric—not neurotic
I would be delightfully daft—not difficult
Original rather than a non-conformist
It would be more comfortable for me and others
So I think I'll be anyway.

February, 1976

A Rose Colored Glass and a Bifocal

Is it enough to be lifted up and let peek through one slat
    of the eternal door
Say on an average of twice a month
And then be set back upon shaky undeveloped legs
And told to go build with blocks and pegs
    something big and real
Which will let you grow tall enough to stand alone
To look through the door?

"Oh no, you'll never see it all
      But if we can only teach you how to look
      and see for yourself!"

But you want Beer and Atmosphere.
You want hands on watches that do not move
And tower clocks that never chime.
You don't want ever moving time.
You ache for a sensuous existence
That calls not for discipline or resistance

Ann Lovell Rowe

Shaving lotion and perfume
Noisy people in a crowded room
You want to dig your polished fingernails
    into expensive tweed
And dance within the circle of the firm and leading arms
    to music that will never last a year
But you don't care—you won't be there to hear it then.

No loneliness or strain—and true no enlightening ecstasy
Just muted minutes, muted minutes without expectancy.

But with a sob you realize
That this could never be--
That minutes are not muted
Hands do move and chimes do ring
Jobs want to be done and people need to be loved
And then too books must be read—and written

A chapel talk, a requiem
A poem, a century
Excite you for a moment, and then slip down into the
    unconscious reserve
While you continue to prepare.

College, 1955

The Fog

You can walk alone with the fog
    So why should anyone condemn it?
Oh, to be secretly enclosed for a minute,
    Enclosed by nature's whisper.

How wonderful to have it all around me,
    Forever protecting me from a world
    I don't like anymore.
No people in that fog.
    Just fog, and me walking.

New Jersey, 1955

Ann Lovell Rowe

Morning Mist, Kirkbridge, Poconos, PA 1984

REMEMBRANCE OF SPRING PAST

SEASONS PURGE and inspire.
Between the intensity of winter and maturity
I am reminded of last spring.

One day I wore a white skirt, a blue jumper,
    and white sneakers.
I was sunburned and warm.
The afternoon sun still danced with the green leaves
While the shadows instructed them.

New Jersey, 1955

Ann Lovell Rowe

Early Romance

If it be true that God made us apart
    To be together,
What mortal then can give the other criteria?
An art, a mission, an environment,
Don't seem to be a basis of interest,
Yet they would take them first,
And then add
    Love.
A minus or a plus?

If man be man only through woman,
And woman find completion only thus,
Why then should we doubt the quality of mystery?
Mystery that asks for nothing, gives no explanation,
Yet gives the answer, "one flesh."

College, 1955

WANTING TO BE

IT WOULD be nice to have summer,
And be warm in the sun.
But sometimes spring comes to the winter,
And it is nice to be warm in the cold.

It would be nice to paint,
But I can only write a poem.
Just as a woman wants to *be*,
But only tends a simple home.

How I long to be someone
    Not me
How sad to be me.
It would not be boring to be someone who is great,
But I could not be that someone,
    And so I wouldn't be at all.

New Jersey, 1955

Ann Lovell Rowe

My Woman's Treasures, Santa Fe 2002

Growing Up—I

I WANT to have children and read nursery rhymes again,
I want to get married so I can make recipes in magazines
    come true
I want to walk into stores and have clerks call me
    "Madame," and have evenings with nothing to do
    except read books in front of the fireplace—
    with someone.
I want shaving cream in the bathroom and
    newspapers at breakfasts.
And I want days empty just to be put together by me.

But I can't have these things now.
I have to study, because
    I'm not grown up yet.

College, Ohio 1956

          Ann Lovell Rowe

Reflections, Austrian Alps 1985

GROWING UP—II

THERE IS a way to know that you're grown up.
The day plus week plus month that you have
    Ached inside and no one has known
Is the day that suddenly you aren't ever really
   young any more.

When you're old enough to reason
And to know inside your mind why you shouldn't be,
And still are afraid—you are old.

The day you play all day among books and people
    And pictures and still know that you are so tight
    inside you can't sleep
That minute that day when you have been projected—
   all relaxed—holding yourself there
   in secondary reality
Only to slip a split second of that minute back to
   the misery of yourself

You wonder at the person
   who has to run away for a whole lifetime,
And it is enough to make you cry
   over all the sorrows that send her running.

College, Ohio 1955

Ann Lovell Rowe

ARROWS AND FEATHERS

LIKE AN arrow
Purpose shoots through a woman's life
With a spear that will shatter mediocrity
And a feather that brushes the Loveliness
    of art on the soul

Europe, 1957

Autumn at the Shore

Call it not September yet
When the ocean swims warm upon the shore
And one is still left with a walk in the waves
And the old men still fish at night.

Call it perhaps an unknown night,
And leave the leather barstool and your beer
The unsound boardwalk
And the tired vacationers and their smells
Far away.

If someone's dog chases you away from the night,
Don't mind, but sit perhaps quietly under the boardwalk,
And suppose, if you're wet,
It will be nice to be dry.

Then as you go back past the old post stuck in the sand
Don't be surprised at the moon
That happened while you were under the boardwalk.

Ann Lovell Rowe

Take a piggy-back ride, topple in the sand
And run till you are breathless
And imagination is caught for one exciting moment.
Without a fear and all belief
Start the walk to the moon
Hardly knowing the warm rolling waves under you all.

Friends' hands on your shoulders,
True pioneers, the moon is really moving to you,
When the wave hits
And your old trained inhibitions chase you back,
     exhausted,
With a smile for silliness.

Wet and happy, resting on a post,
With the pressure of someone heavy resting on you,
     and the post,
You let the wind whip the coldness of you,
And you're glad you are tired.

Bayhead, N.J 1956

HOMEWARD

IN THE smooth sea
The homeward ship goes forward into the night
And I await the lights
And lift my face to the clouds
And remember.

To pray, for me, is to ask
Yet tonight I lift my face in gratitude.

I was given a year
And at last I can say thank you
So that I should only know
If I might take this year
And give as was given to me
As one gives a golden talent
Or returns a fortune.

I will not boast but only, always, ever
Eagerly share and give back
This beauty of a lifetime.

Ann Lovell Rowe

From my place on the deck I see the horizon.

The experiences of a year

Drop to the level of a picture-book wonder.

And all the moments are stimulus

Initiating the plunge into the rest of my life.

And I collapse in gratitude.

Aboard the *Arosa Kulm*, July 1957
Bound from Europe to the USA

Window Reflects Window, Santa Fe 2001

HONEYMOON

WE HAVE a bed that is just——right
Where we sleep
And I curl against Dick
    and he is soft but straight and solid.
We wake in the morning and our whole bodies
    smile at the softness of our love
And the comfort of our sleep.
Tennis, swimming and sunning are all abstractions
We reach toward them but are lost
    in holding on to each other.
Desire and searching gradually we meet each other
    again and again and reassure each other that we are
    married and life slowly slips into place.
And the sand begins to feel beneath our feet
And take on something solid that is us.

Ann Lovell Rowe

We drive from the beach along the coast into the forest.
African living meets us and means our life here to us
Content always to return to dinner and the shower
 and formality of good clothes
 to take Dick's arm and to sit looking at him
 to hold his hand, be thankful,
 to drink the first bit of wine with some kind of pledge:
  Simplicity in our home
  Fulfillment in the evenings
  Completion of our days.

To eat slowly and deliciously,
To go back to our room to read Genesis,
To pray a tired thankful prayer.

I remember how going to bed
 seemed to symbolize marriage
But here I find what is most delicious
The waking up to that face beside my pillow.

Cameroon, 1960

BEING PARENTS

THIS IS a very precious and fragile time for us.
We come together in our love,
    and Peter transforms it.
Yet we both walk unsteadily with ourselves
    and with each other.
Tears come to both of us very easily.
Dick prays very hard to God for His presence with us
    and for His guidance.
We remember that a year ago
God gave us the gift of each other,
God has been with us all year,
    helping us to grow towards one another
Now we are blessed with this new love
    and gift of Peter.

                        Cameroon, March 21, 1961

Ann Lovell Rowe

A Birthday Wish

MAY YOUR joys be as unpredictable
As the number of petals on a daisy!

May your warm feelings as uncountable
As leaves in a pot of tea!

May your years be as noted
And yet as undetected by scrutiny
As the French violets in this potpourri.

May 3, 1975

SHADE AND SHADOW

WE LIVE in a dirty place
The roads are dirt
When it is day there is dust everywhere
It covers the green forest leaves at the side of the road
The leaves then have two colors
   dark green underleaf, finely sprinkled red on top
But you said the dust was everywhere

Cars go by and dust flies into eyes,
   covers the body and sometimes makes a cough

Those in the cars are better off
Unless another car passes them

Everything is green and brown
Except once in a hundred places there is a
   small yellow or red flower
You can take a walk
Down a dirt road past mud villages
One out of every hundred is neat or freshly white-washed
The others are like the dirt, their substance
The roofs of thatch slide or sag
The walls crumble or gape

We can walk down a city street
The buildings are splashed dirty
Their white-wash or paint fades too quickly under the sun
There are no show windows to the stores
Only big barn doors
Open wide when open
Shut when shut

A little girl's hand is very soft
Her eyes very brown in her brown face
Her smile as curved as the roundness of her face.
Is there beauty in a day of celebration
    with dancing and rhythm?
Is there the cool beauty of walking towards a fountain?
Are there people who love their work?

Ebolowa, Cameroon, 1964

On the Children

WE HAVE today, and today only, to live.
I have known it again and again
I know it today.
This is true for everyone, for me, for Richard,
    for Peter, for Andrew,
And it is true for my Christopher

Mr. Townsend said to me when we first met,
"We have three sons too, I have a Christopher too."
Today two of his three sons are dead,
Burned in the air crash, alone.
One was their Christopher.

My mind cannot stay still from the phrase,
"I have a Christopher too"
    repeating and repeating itself.

Ann Lovell Rowe

Last summer, my Christopher ran behind our car
    as I drove out.
He was pinned under the back tire.
He has only a scar on his leg.
The scar is also in our hearts, when he says,
"When you ran over me, Mommy, I cried and you cried."
He says this often, at unexpected moments,
    and it stays buried in my heart.

Richard travels weekly or monthly on planes.
We live but we live only today.
Tomorrow is unknown.
I live today without Richard.
We have given our lives to each other,
But we live apart so much that I am very much alone.

Last year, we hit a child on the Addis Airport Road.
We hit him as he raced across in front of us
    to catch a bus on the other side of the road.
He flew in the air.
Richard cried out with more anguish
    than I had ever heard.

The child flew twelve feet in the air,
   and bounced off our car.
He was bleeding and unconscious.
He had two broken legs.
Now he is well and walking.

A PRAYER

God, teach us to live today.
Teach us, your imperfect people,
To live despite the deaths
from our destructive imperfections
Help us to heal the children and ourselves.
Teach us to live only for each day.

Ethiopia, 1971

Ann Lovell Rowe

Family photo, Ethiopia 1971

The Hurricane is Over

The Hurricane is over
   but it has left the world restless.
The beeper of the emergency truck
   sounds continuously night and day
The buzzing saw of the tree surgeons
   cuts away at the fallen giants—
   fallen on all sides but not on us.
The sun returns brilliantly
   only to highlight the disaster.

Montclair, NJ 1979

Ann Lovell Rowe

PLUNGE

I WOULD plunge through the cluttered verbosity
    of my spirit
Into a small dark place
And find there
A quiet ticking or a soft drum
Not heard for many years.

I would breathe there
First on an island of absence
Then with the sunlight that trickles through.

And the moon will rise first
In an all dark night
A thin curve of glow is clear
Fullness uncertain
Eternity or perhaps a question.

Summer, 1975

CONVENIENT SOCIAL VIRTUE

WE LAUGH
But a laughter of sudden revelation
A stab—we are stabbed by the term
    "Convenient social virtue"
Being married is "A convenient social virtue."
Are we *that*!?
I have no virtue as a "convenient social virtue"
I am by nature neither social nor convenient.
I crossed a doorway, a doorway into ultimate destiny.

Or is it the prison our culture has put us in?
What is our crime for convention?
I wanted to love a man with a woman's love.

I wanted the ecstasy and pain of birth.
I wanted to feel and love
   babies against me
I wanted to create a place for children
And to lead children to grow.

Ann Lovell Rowe

I wanted to grow up again with my children
I chose this birthright to my femaleness,
Did I lose my right to be me?

We crossed the doorway
For us a doorway into ultimate destiny

I will remember, Alice.
We turned one night
Through a doorway of non-convenient women
Into the women's bookstore for the feminist poetry reading.

They seemed fierce to us.
The heavy air in the room
Was the same heaviness I feel
In the all-women bridge games or tea parties.
Or now the *sister* meetings.

Oh, granted it was an esoteric air,
But we couldn't breathe, Alice
And the lack of air caused us to droop
With potion-like sleepiness.

We went out and sat together
   on the step of the bookstore
   for a long time and breathed deeply the fresh night air.
We sat in knowledge of our own secrets
And what it was to be a "convenient social virtue."
With a common glance we fled
Down the steps past the fierce women.

We left into the evening
Hurting deeply
Went home to convenient husbands
And the convenient children
And the comfortable clutter
And the evening cup by the fire
And the marriage bed.

Tulsa, 1975

Ann Lovell Rowe

Building Made Beautiful, Salamanca 2001

MEN IN THE MORNING

OUT OF THE beds they come
    Warm feeling and crumpled
    Smelling like being
To plunge into the shower and come out
    Cold and straight
    Smelling like soap

Dropped are the soft pajamas
Donned are the stiff suits and shirts

The body is pushed and pressed behind razor,
    combs and lotions
Into the sharp crisp advertisement look
So unlike the moment before dawn.

Held against a woman still in soft bedclothes
She still feels the warmth of the body about to leave for
The frantic fuss of the day.

Ann Lovell Rowe

She asks, "Why press your being
    into this pressured world?"
She bids, "Choose rather soft clothes,
    sandles, and sunshine."

    Create your world
    Create your cradle
    Create your cathedral
    Carve out your freer place.

        February, 1976

FRIEND ALICE

FRIEND ALICE of the midnight strawberries
        And the clean tennis shoes
Strawberries cleaned in the hours of predawn waking
        Predawn waking—predawn waking
Alice of the strawberries and the cleaned tennis shoes
Shoes covered with mud demanding to be washed
        Before school, before tomorrow, before dawn.
Are the shoes the reason for the waking?

I see you drawn, tired and anxious
You are my mirror, friend.
And I remember how my spirit fades and flutters
Is gobbled up by laundry, angry children,
    collapsing clutter
Collapsing in my lap.

Ann Lovell Rowe

I see you also bright, confident and delighted
I see your wisdom and your achievements.
I know that although you may not be able
     to find today's laundry tickets
Still through the tornado and two moves
You can still find the Freedom Seder litany
For the friend who calls long distance.
I see you an owner of wisdom and a vessel for light
I know that the wisdom and light often arrive between
     midnight and four a.m.

I take heart in the laughter that rings through you
And I would swing with you on that swing
That carries us back and forth in
     the painful process of Living.
You are a rock for me in these hills
We chose to live among.

                              Rich Mountain, 1976

THE BURDEN OF MY NON-ACHIEVEMENT

I OPENED my door, and with it, myself
   to my two professors
My Yeats professor had said,
      "The writing is good, but why is there
      so little of it?"
Scott, the writer in residence, asked,
      "Why is it only when you go away from home
      that you can write?

And I said,
      "Come in and see. That is why I am so empty."

What did they see
   when they looked in my door?

A cat with blood in its urine.
      A soft, beautiful black cat
      That curls so well.
Curls well on everyone
   but ends up on my lap.

Ann Lovell Rowe

They saw a boy with a broken leg.
A big handsome football player
   who looks twenty, but is only fifteen.
So totally capable of taking care of himself
   except when he breaks his leg

They see a nine-year-old who brings
   a lovely drawing to show
And they hear an eleven-year-old playing music
   who interrupts his music to charm them.
   And they say,
     "You have remarkable children.
     They are a credit to you."

And I respond with half vacant eyes
Like empty pages in the writing assignments.

                 Tulsa, 1976

PEAR TREES IN MY WINDOW FRAME

LITTLE PEAR TREES, how can you bear
To release your blooms, so new
So early, before Easter Sunday?

The blossoms feel the ice and cold of winter
Unfinished or unwilling to be
Resistant to leave us alone and alive with Spring.

Your green new leaves wither and shiver
The sky is so gray
Do you remember the crocuses by the waterfall
Covered three times now by snow?
Do they encourage you that new life comes
Even in total winter darkness?

Ann Lovell Rowe

I remember your leaves glistening red
The last to leave us in the fall
Delicious color that stayed with us past all Autumn sun
Wasn't it already December
Christmastime when they passed into the earth
A little time ago, yet a long time ago?

You stand before my window
    and are for me the Easter cross
Beaten and withering, cold and misery
Yet promising with present blossoms
And remembered red leaves

Easter, 1975

CUP AFTER ANGER

AFTER they left
I lifted the white china cup
Filled with meditating coffee.
As I held it
One small crescent of china
Dropped from its pedestal
And shattered on the table
Before me—unexpected and unprecedented.

I remembered
After my screams, my huffs, my slams
That morning in the kitchen of morning confusion
Kind, constant, careful husband of mine
Also unexpected and unprecedented
Slammed my coffee cup on the table
Angry at my anger.

Ann Lovell Rowe

We tell our children
They must not break things
With their mads.
They must carefully expose them—explode them
In suitable ways and places.

Still anger does break its violent way
Through unsuitable means and moments.
It bursts cloudy and gigantic
And leaves behind its traces.
Haunting is the old phrase
"Once broken it can be mended
But the crack will always be there."

So small a break and smaller still
The sound of the broken piece as it falls.
To remember the weight of that anger,
I keep the cup on the shelf and drink from it
    from time to time.

Winter, 1976

Jack's Death

A Sonnet

I COULD not believe the winter in my sky
It came before the Autumn warmth had gone.
Cold were the lips that kissed my cheek that day
Warm was the last smile not known to me as last.

Warmed by the cat curled in my lap
Unaware of the difference in the day.
My feet felt solid, held tight by the sleeping dog
I did not know then that Autumn had slipped away.

And sent instead an unexpected snow
Too soon for a yellow snapdragon brave and live
Crushed now by the grey wind that began to blow
And nudged the bird so ready now to fly.

And so I see that winter is always there
In every sudden death and in every small despair.

December 8, 1976

Ann Lovell Rowe

RUMINATIONS ON THE PATH

TONIGHT I walked down the rocky path toward the reservoir
And passed under the high trees—a grass ceiling—
A path of soft grass with, here and there,
   white foxgloves,
Lovely elegant flowers,
Past the large old rotten trunk,
Smooth and showing off its many colors.

I will soon lose my children to being older.
I need to mother them now, and gain their respect.
I must chart a path, and keep to it.

I picture my children gathered around the table,
All writing in their journals, and me in mine.
Or gathered making music in the living room.
They do these things and I reassure them
And they respect me.
I read to them and care lovingly for them.
How far away my dream is.

Anger, hostility, fatigue are in our air so much.
There must be another way!

Tulsa, 1976

SAD SATURDAY

I DO NOT like you, Death
You come too close
In the coldness of this winter day
Your fingers slink their way
Around my heart
And then you squeeze
Until the tears come with my love.
Both trickle down
Having rolled out
From the side of my eye and heart
The way the puppies rolled
When Ozark. our dog moved in the bed
Unconscious uncontrolled motion.
Helpless I am
Like the helpless puppies
Helpless I am to chase you
Death away.
I am dry and empty
Like the winter sky.
You came.
And so in the dusk of Saturday
We bury the puppies
Beside the third and newest Christmas tree.

January, 1977

Ann Lovell Rowe

Peter and Ozark, Tulsa 1976

To Peter

ONE DAY sixteen years ago I held your head in my palm
    Your body stretched to my elbow
You were *small* - perfect - and demanding.

I offered you my finger and your whole hand grasped it.
    You held onto me needing me, consuming me—
My thoughts, my time, my tasks were you.
You were happiest held in my arms
    or rocked on my shoulder.

Nowadays, sixteen years later I reach up to you—
    to catch your morning kiss
I return the kiss quickly to your shaven cheek.
Quickly is all the time you offer—
    quickly, how quickly you move.

Your body reaches out from me
    Outward to the world
You are *large* with no deception of perfection
    —yet impossible holds little meaning for you
You are capable, handsome, fun
    —and still demanding.

Ann Lovell Rowe

You are leaving me—my thoughts, my time
My tasks are more mine now.
You are like an egret flying full and strong
Sweeping down only occasionally to sit on my shoulder
    or flop on my bed.

    I remember the white cowbirds of Cameroon
    sitting briefly on the cows.

I like it when you sit on my shoulder
Yet we both know
        Only in the flying will you arrive
        where you are going.

Tulsa, March 10, 1997

Did We Love Him Too Much, Andrew?

You brought him to me and said
"Hold him, Mom and see if he's dead
I may have a dead rabbit, I'm afraid."
I took him on my hand and sat with him and you
Out on the deck in the evening air.
"Let's give him some oxygen,
   some breathing space," I said.
"Maybe I smothered him," you said.
"I was holding him against my chest."

I had agreed, encouraged the holding
Alone from his rabbit family
We thought he needed the warmth and the love.
Someone said afterwards,
"He was a wild creature, you know."
Yet, without the holding we would never have discovered
The large cut, repaired by our vet.

As I held him I said, "I feel something beating."
Hope slipped into our evening breaths.
After some moments I realized and said,
"It's only the pulse in my hand beating."
You took him back to his place on your desk
And we silently agreed not to decide anything that evening.

                                        Ann Lovell Rowe

In the early dawn I could not sleep
I came quietly into your room and looked at his stiff body
You too were awake but we said nothing
Through the early dawn remembering of
Yesterday's streaming Easter sunshine
The lovely small rabbit there amongst the flowers
White and purple violets, lilies and tulips full of new life
You who had no pet, Andrew, had yours now
How confident the vet that the rabbit would survive
How total your promise to pay the bill and care for him
How exciting the choice
In two weeks to let him try again the wild world
Or to make him yours, a pet forever.

Now through it all in my head this hollow cold morning
Through all those hopeful happy moments gone now
I look back and wonder
Did we love him too much, Andrew?
Although you are no wild creature
 you too need breathing space.
In our loving and our holding
Let me give you your breathing space too, Andrew.

Easter, 1977

Moment in Marriage

The air was heavy with the closeness of our living
I felt despair and could not hold your hand
Nor let an arm lie close
Or my head on your shoulder
Or yours on mine
And so I merely slid my finger under your watchband
And let it lie beside the vein in your wrist
The pulses touched
In nodding acceptance
Of that relationship
We chose, called marriage.

Tulsa, Oklahoma
May, 1977

Ann Lovell Rowe

Moment in Marriage, Tulsa 1974

MOVE

I FEEL like a pioneer,
Only moving east instead of west.
The closeness of living frightens me
As the vast open spaces
Frightened my
Frontier counterparts.

Oklahoma to New Jersey, 1977

Ann Lovell Rowe

Moving West to East, Amtrak 1988

Package for Peter

I PACKED you a box today, Peter
    And in it, I put some love
Along with a laundry bag that belonged to Uncle Jim
    When he was in the Coast Guard
I put in a smile between the laundry bag
    And your black Washington tennis team jacket.
    (We are all glad you have your black Washington
    tennis team jacket back.)

And then I put in the extra blanket along with sentiment
    I chose the blue 100% wool blanket that
    Was one of mine when I was younger
Because I know it is warm and I like its soft frayed binding.
It's a comfortable blanket—I wish I could tuck you in.

Tuck yourself in well, Peter (and not too too late)
    and be Comfortable
    —Comfortable

Ann Lovell Rowe

I added the yellow hand-woven Cameroun coverlet
  And with it, I give you a memory—
  A Hausa man from the North Cameroun
  Came to our door to sell it
  And sell it he did, after some long and
  happy bargaining.

Here is your box, Peter
Take time when you put its contents in their places,
Take also the love, the smile,
And the memory.

Montclair, NJ
August 19, 1977

Shade and Shadow—poems and photographs   57

One Woman's Dilemma

I AM trapped
    In the cloak of women's disappointments.
The mothers that I reach out to
Catch me in tea parties and women's associations
    and cooking obligations.

It's become duty, not pleasure.
Requirement, obligation, identity—all these stick to me
Like so many insects from a swamp
And the swamp sinks around me
    And I wade in it.

Montclair, 1979

                Ann Lovell Rowe

Mother's Tea Tray, Santa Fe 1998

MY CHILDREN

MY CHILDREN,
Spin down to your quiet centers.

I want to nourish you to Accomplishment,
to your fulfillments,
your inspirations.
I want to live with you in your order
with our clock by the piano.

I want to encourage your friendships
Pray for you
Support your schools
Bless your joys
Enjoy your music and share your achievements.

My children,
May you spin down to your quiet centers.

Montclair, NJ, 1981

Ann Lovell Rowe

My Children, Pine Barrens, NJ 1979

Watching with a Waiting Hand and Heart

Last night I followed you to the beach, Peter
We were going together, but as often,
You went out ahead, and I enjoyed watching you.

I watched you take the bike onto the beach
    and ride circles on wet sand.
I had a sense your circles were getting larger and larger
    going farther and farther out.

I remembered back to Luxembourg Gardens in Paris
    when you were just a little more than one.
Every afternoon I took you there and let you walk.
I liked seeing how far you would go
    investigating that small world of the park,
    picking up pebbles, touching trees, looking at people,
    patting benches and sometimes people
    with your hands.
It was already a happy game to see how far
    you would go before returning to me.

Ann Lovell Rowe

The other night I watched you go ahead, riding your bike
    on wet sand just before the waves.
I would never think to ride my bike on the wet sand.
I would be afraid it was not good for the bike
    or that I would sink into the sand.
But it was my own adventure watching you dare
    to do just that.
I watched you go where I wouldn't go.
We will watch you go Peter—where we ourselves
    won't go.

Dad was behind us, at home, studying,
    waiting for our return.
He is there, Peter, waiting for you, or on his way to join you.

I am still there behind you,
    ready for the hand of the boy in the Paris park
    who came back to take my hand,
    standing behind the boy-man at the beach,
    who after making his circles on the beach,
    sat down to remember Tulsa with me
    to watch the waves and smoke a cigarette.

Bastille Day, Montclair, 1979

CHRISTOPHER'S FACE ON THE PILLOW

I WATCHED Christopher's face
On the pillow last night
Features being transformed
Before my eyes

Not just the voice
Which we heard changing
Or the biggest feet in the family
But the shape of the nose
From soft to hard
The texture of skin,
The mustache hairs

It was like watching chemistry experiments
Of changing matter into other form
The sensitive soft boy was dissolving
And a firm, defined face
Replacing him.
But not quite yet a man.

Montclair, 1979

Ann Lovell Rowe

Christopher with honeysuckles, Tulsa 1971

Mid-Century

We hung there at mid-century, holding hands and
  coffee cups
And looking at our window.
  Our window hangs there every morning
Like a framed painting but changing with the season.

In winter it had the black bare branches of winter trees
With the pink, lavender sky of winter sunrise.

Now spring has come
We have watched it, first buds,
  then lacy Chinese-looking trees,
  now full green maple.

With the leaves, the sky, the background landscape,
  has changed to full blue
Brightened by yellow early spring sunrises.

Ann Lovell Rowe

However, this morning is different.
A gray heavy cold rain in May
　　has filled and folded back the leaves,
　　they are heavy and dark,
There is no different background
only more heavy,dark sky.

I hold your hand as you start your fiftieth year
I feel heavy, heavy with the years and fearful
　　of the few left.

I would love you still—with—fresh—abandon,
I would seek forever
　　to return to the quiet moments of vacation,
　　of full honeymoon delight
I fear the vision slips beyond,
　　behind a long road whose end disappears
　　out of focus.

　　　　　　　　　　　　　　Montclair, NJ, 1979

I Have Forgotten How Much
I Love November

I HAVE forgotten how much I love November,
   my birthday month.
I've forgotten how beautiful November is.
Perhaps I've forgotten my own life's beauty.
There are still especially magnificent qualities
about November.

The leaves are still yellow on many trees
   and some are still red
And yet the trees also stand a little barren, a little exposed.

More light comes in from the winter light.
The winter light is a very cold light, a bright clear light.

I love the mist that hangs in the air more frequently
   in November than any other time,
   mists that are both mystery and a bit magical.
I've forgotten how especially green pine trees look
   in November
 When they are contrasted to the last yellow leaves.

Ann Lovell Rowe

And in my garden, one red rose.
Can a rose in November be truly a last rose of summer
When summer supposedly closed its door in September?

I've forgotten how much I like November,
    how much I like the leaves all over the ground
    and in the streets sticking everywhere
    and being something to shuffle through
    if you are in the woods.
The leaves are clearly not gone in November,
    they are still with us.

I think I may die in November,
Not this November, but when I do die,
I would like to die in November.
I would like to die with the leaves quietly,
    gently going to sleep.
I would like to die in the month of Thanksgiving
    when we stop to remember all good things.
I would like to die in the month of November,
The November of my birth.

Montclair, 1979

Shade and Shadow—poems and photographs

Haunting Days

All the words of my heart
lie on this small paper you hold in your hand.
I am still as you read it
because none of me is here in this body.
All of me is there on this paper
you hold in your hands.

I MISS YOU, day after day, these days,
I long for something real from you.

The new power I see and feel in you,
I have waited, pushed for, prayed for.
I love it and want to be close.

But when it comes, it is hostile toward me.
And I am here, small, lost alone with myself.

I wave to you from a far beach
And say, "It is me."
Really me, the me you first loved
The me you have loved
As I have grown and changed.
But you refuse to see me.

Ann Lovell Rowe

You see the "me" you have made me in your mind.
And your actions/non-actions
Your unwanted master
(always-wanted mistress)

Your other part—woven throughout
    these years into yourself
    the dependent part.

I turn from that
But you catch me, hold me in the trap and hate me for it.

I run, I lie alone full of afternoon desire to be truly loved.
So long have I desired to have my shoulders gripped by you
And have you truly love the "me" you penetrate.

I fantasize as I drift away in these days of your
    coming coldness.
I fantasize that you will want or need to truly woo
    and court me,
        to make it truly right again.

I fantasize romance, that dance
Of my ever-whining pleading, no longer pleaded for.
I fantasize: caught in your fingers
Pulled by your hands, calling me to dance
    and to love you again.

    "We must be quick, our lives are ticking away
These minutes are our only ones to lose."
You say casually to Christopher about honeymoons,
"Only very few are lucky to have one at Kribi."

We were so lucky, so special.
"It's got to be good" seems lost or far away.
You hold it there on your shelf.

No taking or reaching can make it mine.

                July 5, 1980

                Ann Lovell Rowe

Coming of Winter

YESTERDAY WE watched winter arrive.
    Autumn was long and late. In mid-November
    Many trees were still full of color
    Some still green.
Then for two days a wind howled, and it was very cold.
    Now the trees are bare.

This morning in the early light
    All the branches are bare against the winter sky
Etchings—I love them every year
    And am always surprised when it happens
I want so much for the colored leaves
    To stay on the trees every fall.
I cling to them and the warm days of Indian Summer
    And then I'm always surprised
At how spectacularly beautiful the bare trees are,
And how fresh the winter air is.

Can old age be like this?

Montclair, 1979

The Movable Boulder

I ASKED, "Are you awake?"
You answered, "Yes, but I don't want to be."
And you went back under the covers,
One giant old boulder.

I play with that boulder,
Tickle it, touch it, hold it, shove it.
Sometimes I would like to kick it, but I don't
Or smash my fists against it, but I don't.

I could not smash that boulder
I would not crush that boulder.
That boulder is very strong and very powerful
And it is so solid in its giant grayness.

Ann Lovell Rowe

Is it like the stone in front of the tomb?
Who can roll it away?
What will we find that it is covering?

Not an empty grave,
I think perhaps a plant
An Easter Lily must be there as a bulb
Buried under that boulder.

Pine Barrens, August, 1980

Andrew Leaving Home

Out of the window of our new house
Beyond the neighbor's pear trees
I see that leaves have already
Started to turn
And yet it is still early August

So it is with your growing up, Andrew
You are already there
And the time feels too soon for me

Just as your piano practicing
    Is pure pleasure to listen to
Just as you have only this year
    enjoyed the Times crossword with your Dad

Now that your conversation challenges our thinking
    And the books you read are ones we share

Ann Lovell Rowe

Now that you can cook a fish with a delicious sauce
And because you can waltz me around the room
    To erase my anger, lift my spirits
    with a truly perfect dance step

You feel ready to take the giant step of leaving
You say it is time for you to go away to school

You are sixteen, handsome, charming, articulate, amusing
    We live in joy these days
    And count ourselves lucky for each day with you

                          Montclair, 1981

Andrew, New York City 1984

OUR HOME NO LONGER

TONIGHT I sat for a short time in our car
In front of the house where we used to live.
I looked,
Embarrassingly shy,
At the windows.
Other curtains there, stained glass gone
The wall upstairs seemed painted white
Lost is the lovely yellow.

As I sat there feeling nothing but deep longing,
Suddenly the windows and the door
And the front steps
Seemed to lean toward me,
Like a living thing
The way our dog leans toward me sometimes
Straining to be closer
To touch me.

Montclair, 1981

Ann Lovell Rowe

Reflection, Hotel St. Francis, Santa Fe, 1999

ON THE DEATH OF YOUR DAUGHTER

O JEREMY O Jeremy
I weep for you
I hear Jesus saying
Oh Jerusalem, O Jerusalem
How I have wept for you—
And I think how you have wept for Lark.

I ache—ache
Thinking of you
Gone she is truly gone
Now from you
So many years of reaching and yet not touching
Prayers caring gifts
Love poured out—yours and George's.

I am cold and clammy
With sadness Jeremy
I think of you and wonder
Does it help at all?
All you have learned professionally
All your work helping people to understand
And to face death
All the times you've sat with people

Ann Lovell Rowe

Helping holding life a bit for them—
How can we hold you in *life* Jeremy?

You have become more precious to me
In these last 24 hours as I hold you
Carefully in my thoughts
I see you sweeping your patio
Surrounded by geraniums
Liking to sweep—
I see you caring for George
And loving life—
I want to hold you in life Jeremy
Circle you with healing light
And bathe away the ache.

I am so sorry so sorry
I weep with you
I hold your hand
And I hold you in life
Jeremy—

Montclair, 1981

My Brother Jim

If HE had lived longer
    My father would have been
    75 years old today

    My father was small
    A shy man with tremendous discipline
    in achieving his goals.
He's gone
    but we are his family—

    I walk through my kitchen this morning,
Glance then enjoy
    the luscious bouquet of fresh flowers—
A birthday present from my brother.

My brother is not my father
He is extravagant and large.
Signs of my brother's visit are all around

The freezer has a bag of ice—
    Store-bought ice, "to have enough."
The frig has special deli packages of roast beef and salami,
    Ham and sliced cheese—

    Ann Lovell Rowe

We usually buy one or two for sandwiches
    Generous now we indulge in "more than enough."
The cupboard has *Wise potato chips*
    Lots of them—3 kinds—
No A&P Ripples for Jim

Andrew reads Christmas catalogues
    and thinks about "what I will buy for Uncle Jim"
Asks me my opinion–Doesn't wait for an answer
Then says "I know him well enough to decide"
Knowing "well enough" –Being Home Together

Who we are often skips generations
My brother is not like my father

He is most like my grandfather—
    Talks with his sense of extravagance and luxury
Full of schemes and plans

This makes me wonder
    where the essence of our three children
    find their identities—
In my husband's and my being
    Or in other generations?

November 27, 1981

Time Reconsidered

I CATCH IT, I promise it
I put the clock in front of me
and I write for one hour.

Reality comes sweeping in,
    from the gray, slow-moving clouds
    in the sky, it comes.
The flock of black specks, birds in the sky,
    dance their tune.
The cats play away
    in and out of the frost-bitten flowers.

My magic moments fade. My mental images flee.
My clear, gorgeous, inspired words disappear
    and the thoughts tap away in dull prose.

My fantasies, my inspirations carry me
    so high above so many people
They allow me that privilege of saying life is wrong,
    too difficult for the living.
I will sweep everyone I know
    into ecstatic sunlit visions of new clarity.

Ann Lovell Rowe

But when I put the clock in front of me to write,
It is all quite dull and perfunctory.
The emotions of honest confrontations all disappear,
Not so important after all.
I am somehow disappointed.

I am also more practical
And I rise from the clock
    to do the next thing on my list,
    to say to the day
    "O.K., I'll have you,
    and will hold onto you
    and you will not twist from my grip
    to slip behind my back and bash and baffle me."

I shall march with high steps
Through the minutes *bam bam bam*
And I shall be happy when nighttime comes.

Montclair, 1981

The House Must Become the Haven

THE HOUSE must become the haven
The place of retreat
Tear out the telephone
Turn off the doorbell
Yearn not to go far away
Simply go away only
      For a walk
      A bike ride
      A moment of music
      A story by the fire
      To enjoy the candle burning
Take and keep the last vacation
      Vacate the brain
      Make vacant your place, your head, your soul,
      Your very Self
      And B-R-E-A-T-H-E.
Do not see others, do not think others.
      "Be still and know that I am God."
      Be still and know that you are who you don't know.
      Be still and know that you do know.
Becoming a new creation, Always being created if open
To C-R-E-A-T-I-O-N.

Montclair, 1982

Ann Lovell Rowe

SUMMER'S TRAILS

WE SLIP into summer
With expectancy
Like dew and mists
And hopeful things.
Summer's trails are green trails—
Leading and long
Offering to be taken.
Summer's hours have extra sunlight
Soft morning, early morning dawns,
Late evening hellish red skies
That splatter and explode
And then slip below the horizon.

Pine Barrens, NJ, 1982

Failed Sonnet

My husband and I
    will not destroy each other.
    I have a vision of him seeing me
    and saying, "That is who you really are."

"I denied you your years
    because you would threaten me."
    My part of me in you cannot stand to feel like that
    so I will not stand for you feeling like that!

My friend, do I need so badly for you to approve me?
    Will I topple if in your eyes
    I haven't got what you think
    is necessary for me to be
    re-cog-nized! and *ac-cep-ted!*
    Unlike you I am no sonnet writer.

                           Cranford, NJ, 1985

Ann Lovell Rowe

Two Trees

The tree, because it is old, loses its leaves earlier.
It stands there in the new October at 5:00 a.m.
The Full Moon peers between two old, craggy branches.
And I say to the tree, "So, you are the tree."

It looks back at me.
I see that it is the old Duma tree from Cameroun
Without any of its branches.
The Duma is twice as tall as this tree.
There are no trees so tall in America
Save, perhaps, the Redwoods.

This tree holds hands
With the Duma tree in my heart.

Gone is the wondering where my new images will be.
I have found them in this tree,
In the promise that the old images
Will re-appear and connect with the new.

Cranford, 1985

FOR YOUR GRADUATION, CHRISTOPHER

THE SMILE—awards night.
Four years ago you took to the stage in Showcase
You put on a smile and placed yourself
    before the high school world.

Last evening, for the first time, you danced
    onto that stage again with Vicky
To receive the first of several awards.
That smile was no longer *on* you
      It was all through you
      It came up from your feet and flowed out
      Through your face and hands.

The high school world belonged to you
Throughout the evening.
That same high school world smile at you
Not least of all in the applause and cheers
    from the students, teachers, and parents
    and the warm hugs afterwards.
Your smile owned you and you now
    owned that high school world.

June 21, 1985

Ann Lovell Rowe

Lace in My Days

BEFORE DAWN moments give breath
To the creative thoughts
There that day at dawn
Seeing, searching, looking, waiting on God
If God be there.

Coffee communion with Dick because he is there
Common prayers because we are there
Given another day to bless and be blessed.

Boys all three now enter on stage
In some ways, sometimes
And weave their burlap strings, and their leather cords,
And their piece of wool, and their fine pieces of thin
    colored plastic for weaving into my lace
        And the lace is sometimes broken.

Pick up the strings, All of them
And stretch and swim and dance
And hold the lace to my face and let the tears flow.

Cranford, NJ, 1987

I Could Not Leave

I MET an old boyfriend,
By a most astonishing accidental coincidence.

And so we began to see each other
Quite harmlessly in terms of infidelity
But with delightfully delirious times.

Laughter, appreciation, more laughter
A drink, a folk-tale lecture, the gift of a book,
Walks and talks.

I felt embarrassingly guilty
Each time when I got home.

The last time
I came home to bed
Moved against my husband's back.

Ann Lovell Rowe

I felt the fullness of his body against mine.
And all the layers of living filled the spaces
Between us.

Memories of years of common experience
Filled my heart
And I know I could never leave
Our marriage.

Cranford, 1986

FOSSILS FROM ANGER

WAVES OF anger sometimes wash—
    As do the waves of the sea
Leaving on the shores of our souls
    Fossils of our feelings
Our faults—or the fault of the other—or life's fault.
The reasons for the anger
    Can lose some of their edges
    Even take on smoother softer shapes
    Because of the raging sea
Or the thoughtful somber aftermath of the anger
    Which tosses these stones of our spirit
Slowly continually spinning and looking and feeling
  the hurt
    Until it settles on the shore of our spirit
    As a changed piece—a new object—
    A fossil of anger
Think of a shore with its crab shells and pebbles,
  rocks, and other carcasses
    Then, think of the pieces of anger and hurt
    Like stones in an oyster—
Can they be a pearl of new insight,
A newer, fresher closeness?

Venice, 1985

Ann Lovell Rowe

SITTING IN A PARIS CHURCH

CLEAN OUT my heart, O Lord,
Scrape it clean to do the loving it needs to do
Clear it empty of rancor, regrets, and despair.

My heart is old and burdened,
Scrape out my fears and tears
And leave my heart clean and open to love again.

Paris, October, 1983

MEDITATION ON MARRIAGE

THIS SUMMER there were two instances
   when the substance of our marriage
   was regenerated for me.
One was at the time of our dog Ozark's death.
Dick brought out *The Little Prince*
   and read to me two very special passages
   that touched my soul.
The second time was when he brought home a book
   for me by Meister Eckhart, "mystic and
   philosopher,preacher and theologian,
   administrator and poet, spiritual genius,
   declared heretic."
We have been reading it in early morning musings
   during our tenting time.
If I were looking for a symbol for our marriage,
      I have found it today.
      It is the ability to touch each other's souls.
Dick won my heart in Cameroun
      When he both read to me *Le Petit Prince*
      to teach me French
      And when he prepared a birthday party for me
      with a reading of T. S. Eliot's *Murder in the Cathedral*.

This is how our Souls touched,

    With images and ideas,

    Sharing our beliefs in life

    And the mystery beyond life—God.

God is the most precious part of what we both

    have held in common

And our view of God that we have shared

    and offered one another.

From the soul's touching

    comes the assurance to risk all in marriage.

Then, one of life's dances begins

With all the symbiotic pains and pleasures,

The gifts and tensions they arouse.

    From jealousy to dependence,

    From frustration and blame

    To retreat and disappointment,

    From blame to dependency,

The cello plays and the strings make music

And then screech in disharmony and anguish.

Pine Barrens, 1987

THE OLDEST

IT SEEMED I had given a part of my life
To make it possible for him to both love to read
And to read well
To read deeply enough
To understand
What I wrote in my newspaper columns
Deep expressions of what I felt and thought
Expressions I could never make verbally
Out loud.

We sat over breakfast in Chicago
I felt all the emotions of love, distance, growing up—
In the few moments we sat there as
I shared my columns with him.

                                        Chicago, 1981

Ann Lovell Rowe

THE FIRE

THE FIRE moves
    from the corner fireplace
Moves across my bed
    and out into the hall slowly
Up each stair step
    warming the corners
And then comes to sit by the sill
    of the closed outside exit door
Wondering where to go next

Santa Fe, 1996

SMALL BOOK

GENTLE SMALL book
Holds for me a new poem
Lovely poem
Connecting us
Touching the book with my fingertips
I love and I feel.

I remember long ago in a house
With no lights we sat on the floor
And read from our favorite poems by candlelight.

Connecting us
Touching with fingertips
The book
And then each other
Fingertips, cheeks, and lips.

Santa Fe, 1998

Ann Lovell Rowe

THE DARK AND HEAVY WINTER SKY

THE WINTER sky sits hard,
    Dark and heavy, bearing down
On the range of mountains visible from my window.
    There is a small strip of light seeping through

Then I sit in my bed thinking and praying.
    The sun breaks through and lightens
The sky in clarity-
    A daytime set of clouds settles in
With my daytime mood
    And on the tasks that take me
Away from early darkness.

Santa Fe, 1998

REMEMBERING RESPONSIBILITY

JUST SO you'll understand
    why responsibility is such a big thing for me . . .
I am the oldest child.
    I always felt totally responsible
    for making my mother feel OK
I was also responsible for making my little brother
    be good and responsible!
I got a lot of gold stars in junior high school
    because I was 'responsible'

    I went to Africa

    because I wanted to 'do more' with my life

Two years later in the delicious moment,
The first morning I was back in our own house
    at the foot of the big hill in the deep rain forest
I held my first child.
I felt flooded and overcome with the reality that
I was responsible
    in a new way——in a total way
    for this tiny boy

Ann Lovell Rowe

Forty years later
I sit in my son's living room
In the chair that was my father's special chair.
I am reading beside a good fire in the fireplace—
a book I've never heard of but find fascinating
I am not responsible
for what we will do or eat.
I have a crushed velvet scarf around my neck
said to eliminate anxiety
since it is filled with lavender.
It is a rare moment at Christmas.

I feel slipping out from the top of my head,
down through the tips of my fingers,
Leaving through my body out my toes, Responsibility.

I am no longer responsible
In this lovely home
Which belongs to that same tiny baby
Now an all-competent forty year old
With a lovely family
Two small boys I treasure

But I am not responsible.

Dallas, December 26 2001

Shade and Shadow—poems and photographs   *103*

PEARLS FOR DANIEL

TWO-YEAR OLD Daniel reached for my long strand of pearls.
    I gave them to him.
    He put them on.
He walked around with the pearls hanging
on his bare two year old chest,
pleased and proud of himself.

His mother Cathy picked him up
And began to dance with him
    Swinging him in big circles.

I picked up my camera
Following their dance
The photos have come back.
    Their beauty charms me.

Cathy in her blue sweater and long hair,
Daniel with my pearls floating over his shoulder
    as Cathy whirls him around
His laughing face looking up
 As the pearls float down to settle on his chest again
And Cathy's long hair floats back around her smiling face.

Ann Lovell Rowe

Christopher sits in the large chair
and watches the happy scene.

Today is Daniel's birthday. He is two years old.
Will he remember somewhere in his deep heart
That I gave him my pearls when he asked for them?

New York, April 20, 2002

At Our Age

WE ARE on a trip with a group
Of people who comment on how
Nice it is to see us holding hands.
(What is not said is, "At your age"
Or, "After all these years.")

But for now I know hands are all important.
In the night, the full, flat hand on my back
Or between my thighs
Warm and connected.

In the day, the touch of fingers
On my back in passing
Or the firm beginning and ending
Of the hard, full embrace in the morning.

The deep sexual organs come alive
From time to time,
But daily these days
It is his hands that care, feel, touch and bless me.

Santa Fe, 2001

Ann Lovell Rowe

At Our Age, Camino de Compostella, Spain, May 2001

Shade and Shadow—poems and photographs 107